Christmas
TREATS & TREASURES

7 Piano Arrangements of Holiday Favorites

Catherine Rollin

Among the greatest sources of inspiration during the holiday season are the beautiful, joyful, and uplifting carols and songs that have become seasonal favorites. I hope that these *Christmas Treats & Treasures* bring many special musical moments to piano students as they celebrate the holidays.

Catherine Rollin

Contents

Alfred Music
P.O. Box 10003
Van Nuys, CA 91410-0003
alfred.com

© 2019 by Alfred Music
All rights reserved. Printed in USA.

ISBN-10: 1-4706-4252-2
ISBN-13: 978-1-4706-4252-5

Cover art:
Holiday icons: © Getty Images / Diane Labombarbe

Angels We Have Heard On High

Traditional French Melody
Arr. Catherine Rollin

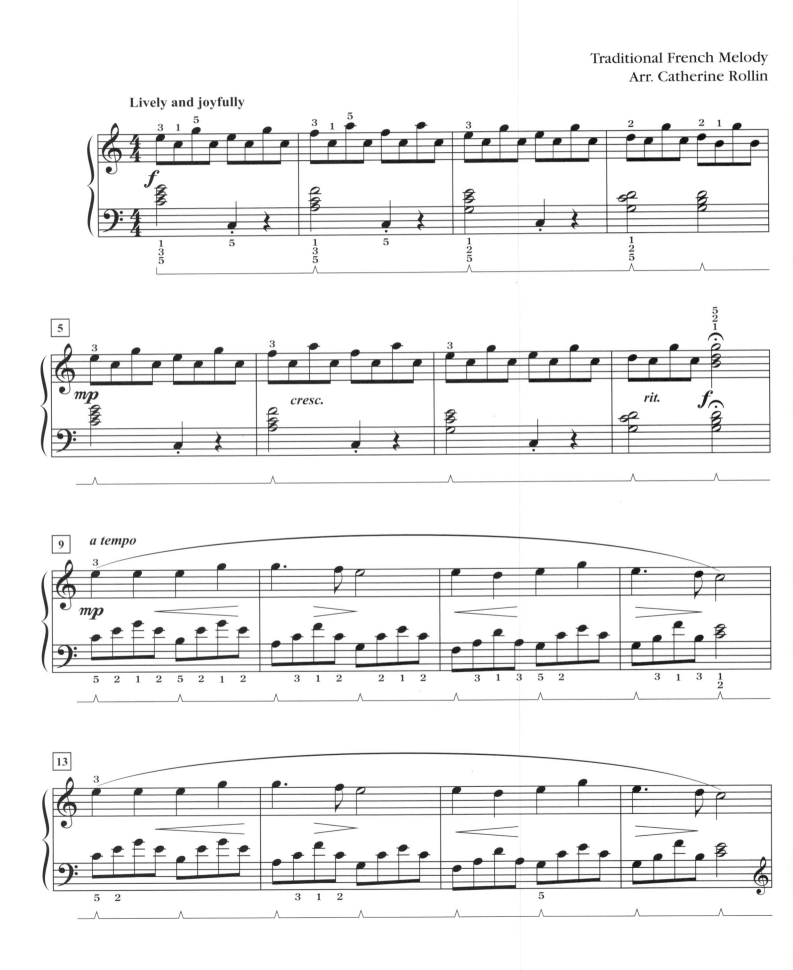

O Little Town of Bethlehem

Lewis H. Redner
Arr. Catherine Rollin

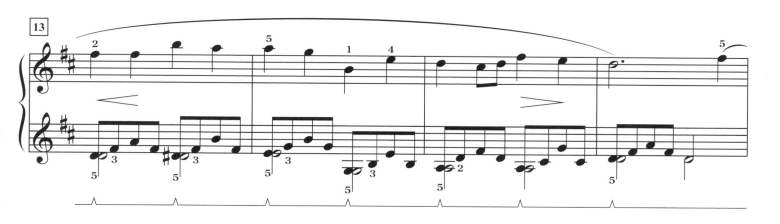

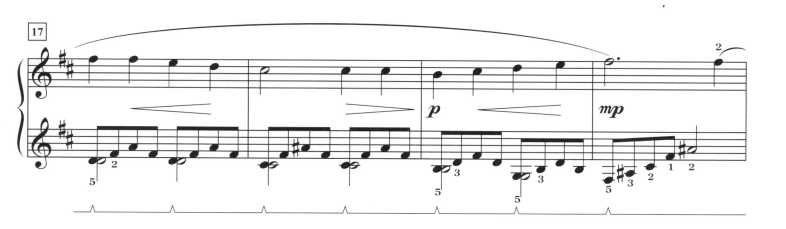

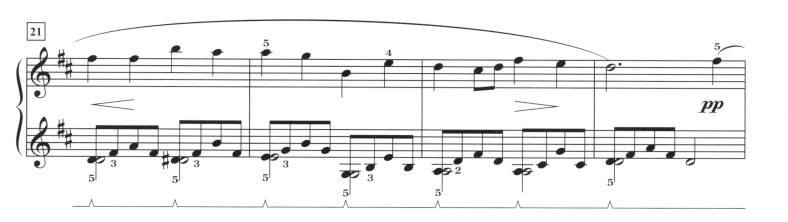

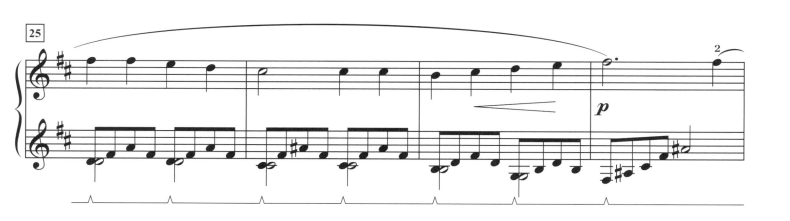

Up on the Housetop

Benjamin R. Hanby
Arr. Catherine Rollin

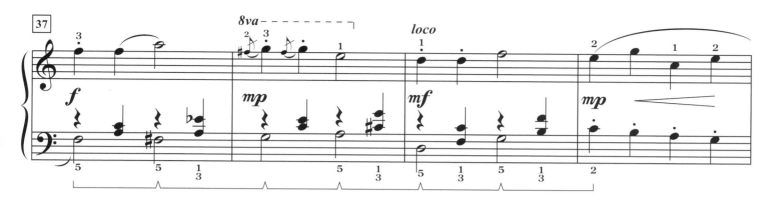

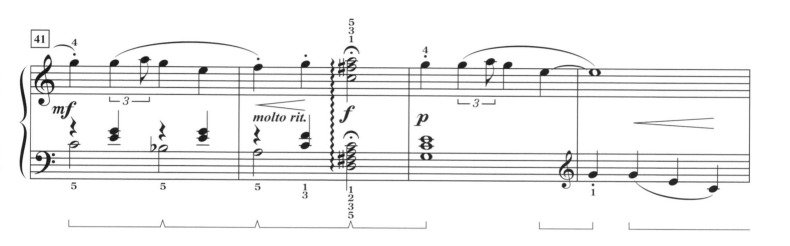

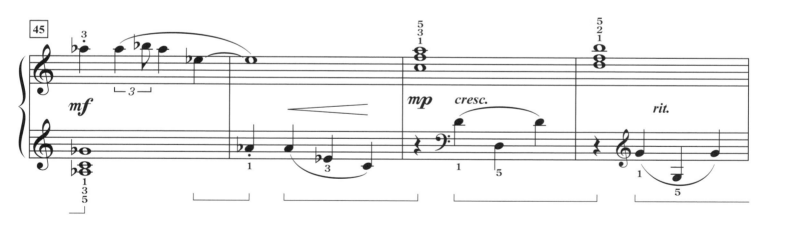

It Came Upon the Midnight Clear

Richard S. Willis
Arr. Catherine Rollin

Jazzy & Jolly Old Saint Nick

Traditional
Arr. Catherine Rollin

Away in a Manger

James R. Murray
Arr. Catherine Rollin

Ukrainian Bell Carol

Mykola Leontovych
Arr. Catherine Rollin

* Bring out top note.